TABLE OF CONTENTS

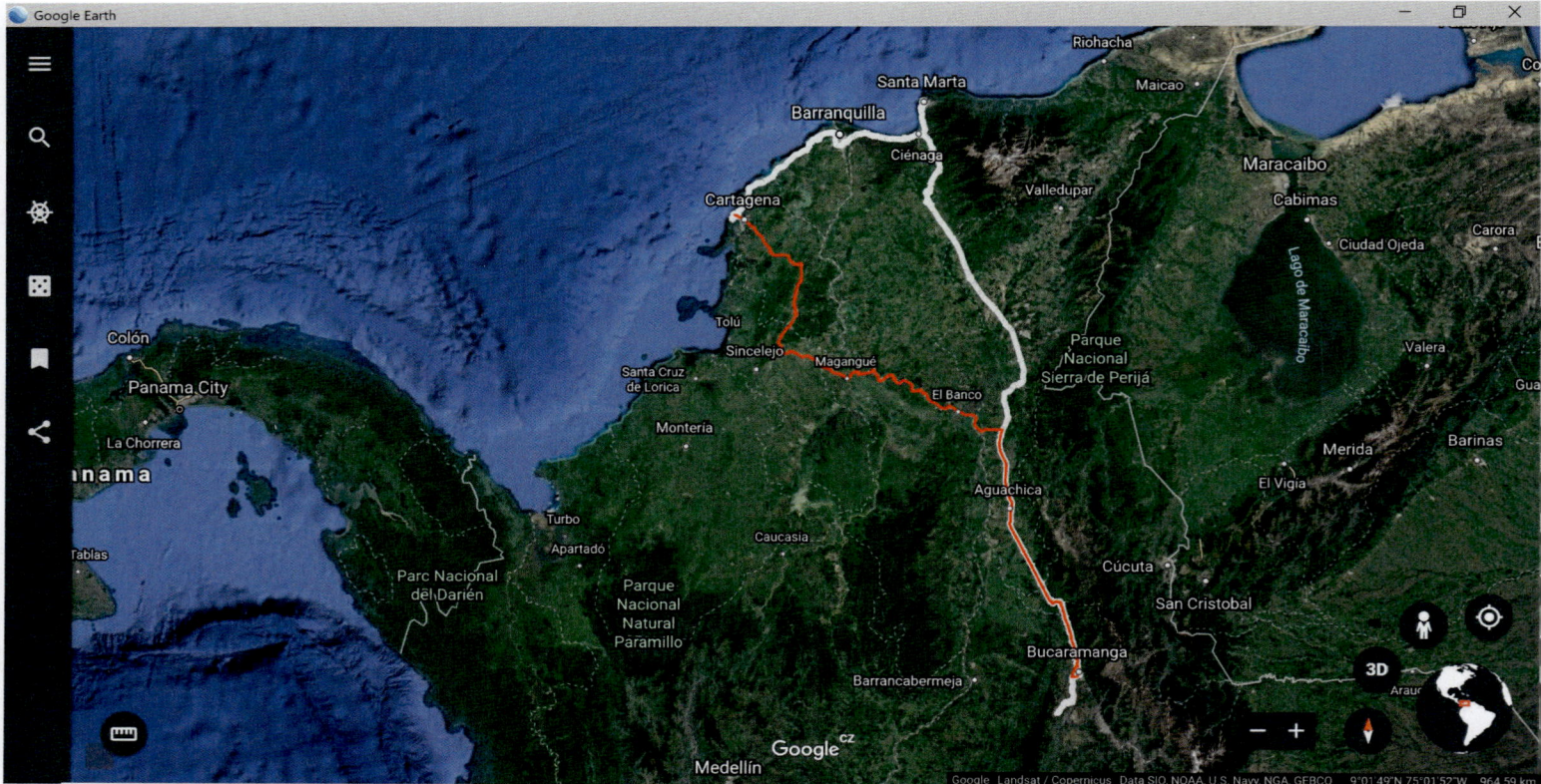

Google Earth Landsat/Copernicus Data SIO, NOAA, US Navy, NGA, GEBCO Google CZ

PREFACE

Long before the rest of Colombia was safe to travel around, tourists dared to visit Cartagena on the country's Caribbean coast. By now, the armed conflict in Colombia has long ceased to hinder Colombia's tourism and tourists venture all over the country.

While most tourists to Colombia visit Cartagena, few travel elsewhere in the north, preferring to skip the idea altogether and head to Bogota, Medellin and the Coffee Country next. That's unfortunate as the north has much to offer and you should consider touring it on a bicycle.

Colombia is a cycling country. Next to football, cycling is Colombia's second most popular sport. You'll see local cyclists on roads all over the country, however, riding a bicycle in Colombia may not be for everyone.

Unless you have bicycled on roads with traffic, Colombia may not be the place where to start. For one, the main highways are busy and carry heavy truck traffic. The roads also lack a shoulder though not everywhere. The tarmac is rarely in the best of shape so you must watch out for potholes. And let's not forget the heat. You wouldn't want to ride during the rainy season, thus cycling in the north of Colombia in the dry season will be a hot affair!

Sounds discouraging? Wait! Even though I noted the main highways are busy hence dangerous, this is Colombia and the drivers, truck drivers above all, are courteous. People at roadside and drivers alike will honk in admiration and support of your effort, give you the thumbs up, and provide you with ample space when they pass. You have heard it, and sounds like a cliche, Colombians are nice people. They are. For that simple reason alone to ponder a bike trip in Colombia is worth the thought.

That's where this book comes in. Northern Colombia by Bicycle is a travel pictorial of a cycling itinerary from Cartagena via Santa Marta, Bucaramanga, Santa Cruz de Mompox and back to the Caribbean coast. Through the photographs, you discover the character of this unique passage.

Organized into chapters corresponding with the bike stages, you ride along the Caribbean, then up the Andes to Bucaramanga and back to the coast crossing the floodplain of the Rio Magdalena and the Maria Hills.

The pictorial will introduce you to the route and the sights, and assess the pros and cons of the trip, thus help you decide if this is a trip you wish to undertake.

Northern Colombia by Bicycle is an alternative way to enjoy this wonderful country. The travel pictorial is your window into the environment and culture and leaves you to contemplate setting out on this journey yourself.

CARTAGENA

Before heading out cycling east along the Caribbean coast, you need to acclimatize to the heat. I suggest three rides, each time getting started at sunrise. My first ride was along the highway 90A to get familiar with the traffic at this time of the day and the road itself. On the way back I rode along the waterfront to Bocagrande, the new highrise studded upscale neighborhood of Cartagena. I did a similar ride on my third day in the city.

Top: Highway 90A in La Boquilla, east of the downtown; no shoulder.

Left: Cycling Bocagrande

Below: Atop La Popa Hill. Cartagena's highest hill offers sweeping views of the city and is a great practice ride from sea level to 150 meters ASL, although the ride through the city and the neighborhood below is not pleasant.

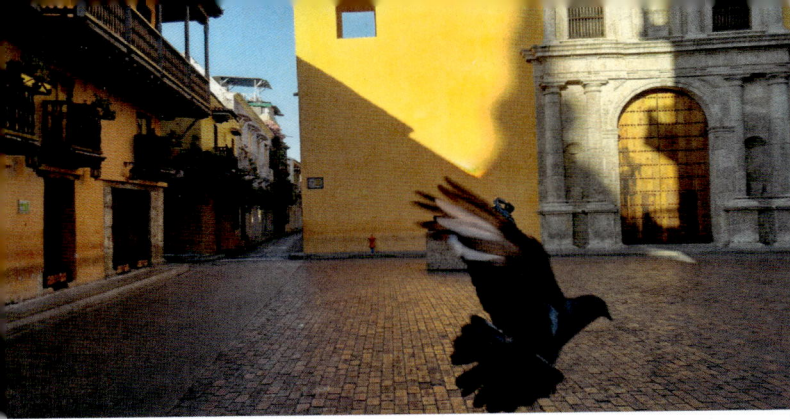

Above: Plaza de Santo Domingo.
The Old City is crowded all day hence the squares,
cobblestone streets with colorful colonial buildings are
best to ride at sunrise when you can have he Old Town
to yourself.

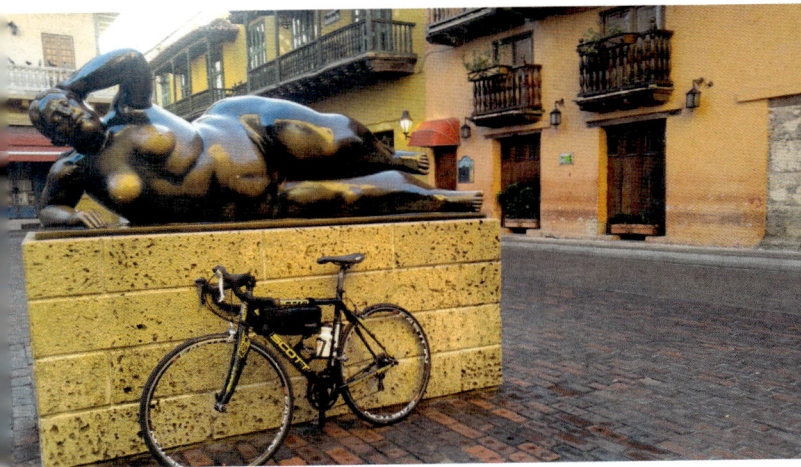

Above: Sculpture of La Gorda Gertrudis by Fernando
Botero in the Plaza de Santo Domingo.

The Old City is crowded all day hence the squares and
cobblestone streets with colorful colonial buildings are
best to ride at sunrise when you can have the Old Town to
yourself.

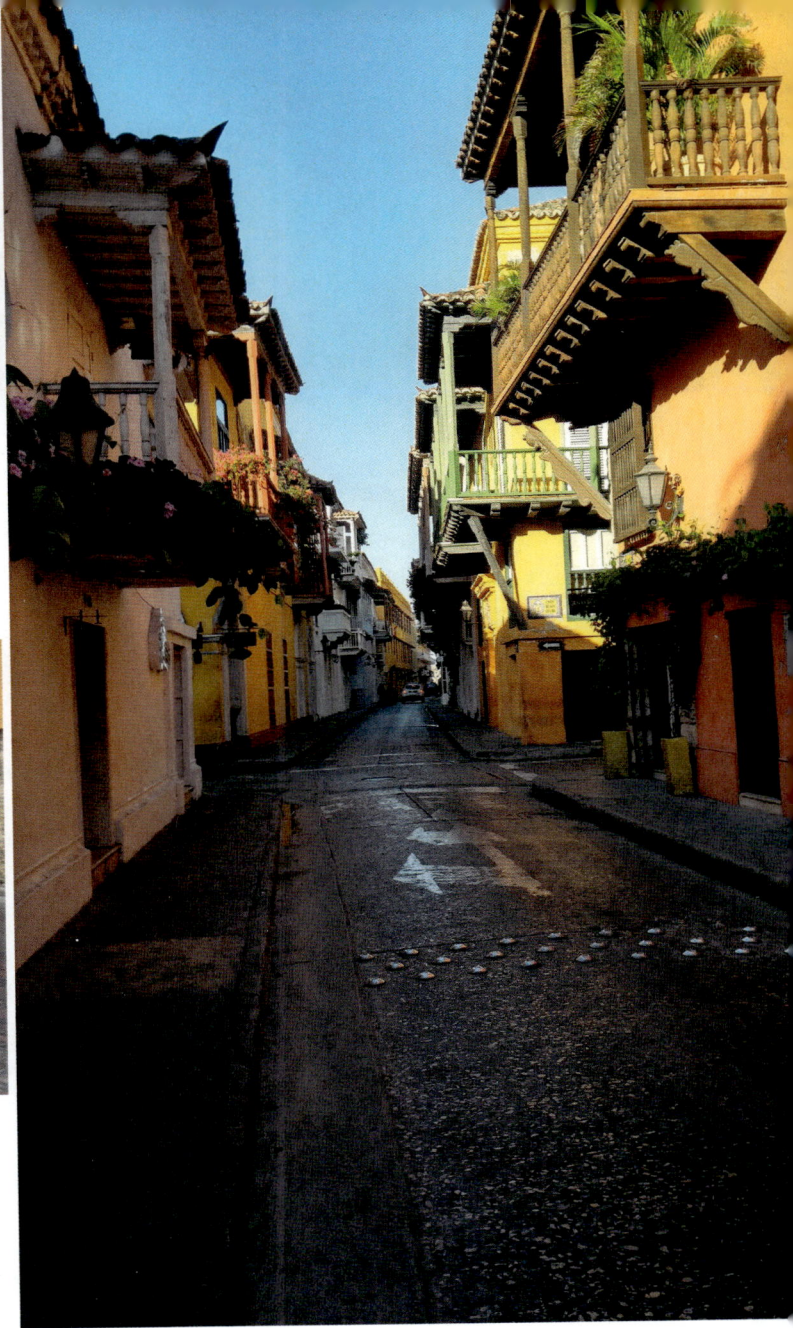

Cycling the Old Town early in the morning.

BIKEPACKING

I expected having to deal with a hot climate in northern Colombia, hence decided against cycling fully loaded, meaning I didn't bring my tent, sleeping bag and cooking gear. This was not to be an expedition-style bicycle tour, not this time.

Expecting heat, I wanted to travel light. From my previous trip to Colombia I knew finding accommodations in Colombia was not a problem, so why bother to bring a tent and camping gear, I concluded.

Instead of touring on my Surly Long Haul Trucker DeLuxe draped with heavy panniers, I converted my old carbon road bike Scott into a light-weight version of a transcontinental bikepacking machine.

Bikepacking has appeared on the scene in recent years namely associated with off-road long-distance bike touring in the mountains. Continental Divide, Pacific Crest and the Appalachian Trail see bikepacking cyclists riding loaded MTBs, hauling all the gear necessary to be self-reliant in remote areas but doing it with no bike racks and panniers. Instead, the bags mount to the handlebars, saddle post and the bike frame.

To ride northern Colombia, I expected to stay on paved roads and brought a race bike strapped with bikepacking-style bags.

My packing list contained only the clothing I wore to ride every day and a set of trunks and a singlet to change into when off the bike. Other than a few gadgets and a rain jacket, I figured I needed nothing else.

I was right, and I could have skipped the rain jacket too as it was super dry, not a drop of rain when I toured.

I brought a simple multi-tool and a spare inner tube, but guess what: I didn't have a single flat riding 1200 km, much of it on a bad tarmac including stretches of dirt and gravel. Riding 25C tires, it surprised me but no complains.

For the essentials, passport, money and another bottle of water, I carried a small day-pack. Road-cycling northern Colombia in February-March, come light!

DAILY ROUTINE

I got on the way each morning as early as 4:45, usually between 5 and 6 AM. Before the first crack of dawn I rode with my headlight on, often until around six. I kept my taillight on much longer. This being February, it was dark until 5:30 AM.

The early start was necessary to get a jump on the heat because the temp was rising quickly. By 8 AM, it was already around 25C. By 10 AM it was over 30C. After 11 AM, it was pushing high thirties. By noon, it was low 40s and getting hotter. The worst time of a day was mid-afternoon until 6 PM.

The highest temps were not along the coast but in the northern plains. Near the sea, however, due to the ocean proximity the air was more humid and stifling.

STAGE 1: CARTAGENA TO PUERTO COLOMBIA

Distance: 109 km

Altitude Profile (-4 m to 116 m)

Two longer and steeper climbs, otherwise shorter punchy ones; the rest is flat. There are no trees to get a shade. It is a scorching introduction to cycling northern Colombia! Beware, by 9 AM the headwind picks up, for which the Caribbean coast is well-known.

Below: Watch out for anteaters!

The first stage from Cartagena to Puerto Colombia was the hardest. The heat overwhelmed me despite the three days of rides in Cartagena. The stage was the longest of the tour for a reason - there is nowhere to stay east of Cartagena until Puerto Colombia; the next option is Barranquilla. I learned that the only sensible routine was to get on the way early and finish early. I wanted to get in by 11 AM, no later than noon. I was a little late on my first day and paid for it. Cycling past noon that extra hour made a lot of difference - I still had water but it was boiling and dehydration hit me severely. Below: In the post-colonial era, Puerto Colombia was the country's main port on the Caribbean coast where European immigrants entered the country. Today it is a sleepy small town, in February offering a windy beach but spectacular sunsets.

2: PUERTO COLOMBIA TO CIENAGA

Distance: 96 km

Altitude Profile (-1 m to 88 m)

In the beginning of the stage, there are several steeper climbs, maximum 80 m. Once in Barranquilla and from there on the rest of the way at sea level.

COVERED HEAD TO TOE

After my first day, I realized that I had to ride covered head to toe, face included. My three days of day rides in Cartagena, I rode unprotected, in shorts no tights, nothing on my face, save a little of sunscreen. After I got to Puerto Colombia, I knew better. Sunscreen wasn't enough.

From that point on, I rode in my long tights, a long sleeve t-shirt or arm sleeves, and a tube-scarf pulled right under my glasses. Without, when I was riding on the narrow strip of land that separates the Ciénaga Grande de Santa Marta, a mangrove swamp lagoon and the Caribbean Sea en route to Cienaga, the temperate on the sun was pushing 50C and the heat effect on my face wearing nothing felt as if I'd be facing a steaming spout of a teakettle. Never mind, I looked like a bandit. It saved the skin on my face from blistering, literally.

On the bike year round, my legs stay brown but I still felt inclined to wear the tights in northern Colombia, and I did the entire trip, when on a bike.

It didn't cool off until I climbed from the plains past San Alberto, but the sun was still merciless and stayed that way even in the altitude of Bucaramanga.

In was hot in the plains and even more so in the floodplain of the Rio Magdalena, and it never let up. I rode in the same killer heat full-circle back to Cartagena.

WHEN TO GO

That said, is February a good time to come and ride the route I did? Actually, the dry season at its peak is December-January, so February is already somewhat of a shoulder season before the wet months of April-May set in. From my experience, August-September is good too, perhaps cooler, but the downside is it will rain more often, even if not continuously. And with even a little rain, it will be a factor, namely the humidity. I prefer the dry heat. Cartagena and the Caribbean coast is hot all year; most visitors come between December and March.

Below: Now snakes to watch out for... Just saw another cyclist swallowed by a giant anaconda, including his bicycle... (just kidding)

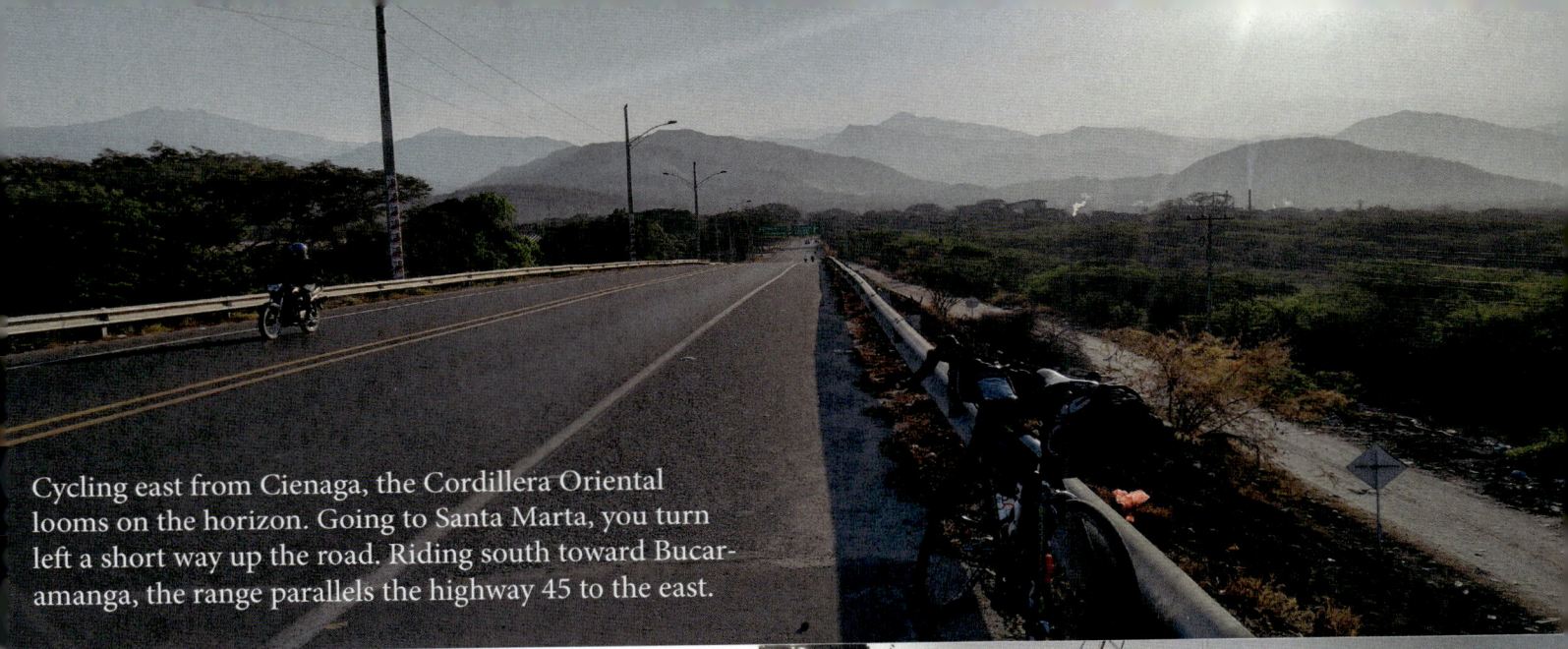

Cycling east from Cienaga, the Cordillera Oriental looms on the horizon. Going to Santa Marta, you turn left a short way up the road. Riding south toward Bucaramanga, the range parallels the highway 45 to the east.

3: CIENAGA TO SANTA MARTA

Distance: 43 km
Altitude Profile (1 m to 103 m)
Short climbs up to 50m elevation rise, then twice that from Rodadero to Santa Marta crossing a ridge between the two towns.

Below: a panorama of the barrios below the pass, the downtown of Santa Marta in the distance.

Bottom left: Awesome sunset at the Rodadero Beach.

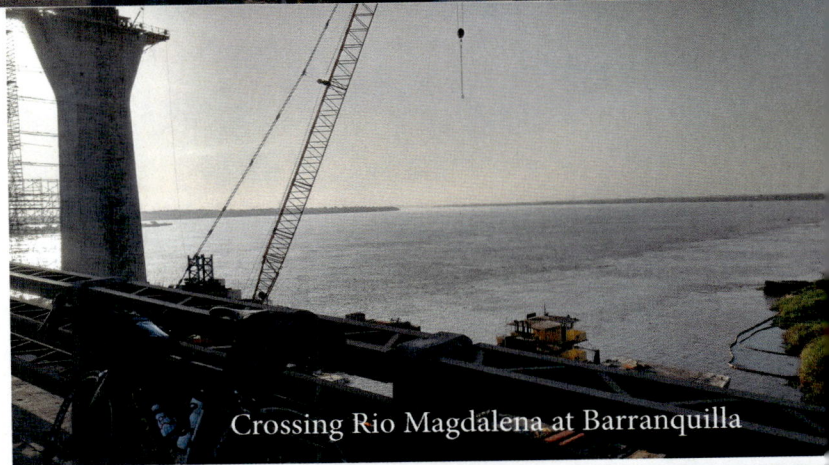

Crossing Rio Magdalena at Barranquilla

4: SANTA MARTA TO FUNDACION
Distance: 92 km
Altitude Profile (2 m to 55 m)

Pleasant stage with lots of trees and views of the mountains, a great respite after the heat of the coastal route 90A. This is banana country, plantations on both sides of the tarmac. Now on the highway 45, the principal artery between the northern coast and Bogota. Barranquilla and Santa Marta are the key traffic sources, and the traffic is steady. There are trucks, big trucks, monsters, Macs to Volvos and any other brand, often a whole train, maybe a dozen traveling one after the other, their engines roaring just past you, but it goes in spurs and the drivers are courteous. Right: New sign: Watch out for beautiful Colombianas with big eyes and long eyelashes up ahead! (just kidding again)

FOOD

By now, I became accustomed to the food choices available. Although I dreaded the sight of the meat at first, the deeper into the interior of Colombia I cycled, the more I appreciated the "plato del dia," the fixed menu lunch, the typical "almuerzo." The most nutritious was the soup as the broth contained often lots of vegetables. The main course was typically a slab of meat. As I conquered the routine and ate lunch after I finished cycling for the day, hungry as I was, I craved my daily dose of the carnivorous feast.

For dinner, I frequented the streets for options. I did not want to repeat lunch nor was it usually available. This time of the day, the street carts proliferated. The way to find the best of the "empanadas" or any street food was to scan the streets for where lined up the locals. While I usually started with two beers, after I ate I'd always have a glass or two of "jugo naturales,"guanabana being my favorite. Colombians love sugar and so you always have to alert the juice preparer not to put any in your glass!

5. FUNDACION TO BASCONIA
Distance: 73 km
Altitude Profile (46 m to 183 m)
Grab a cup of coffee and "arepa de huevo" at one of the
stalls along the 45 catering mainly to truckers.

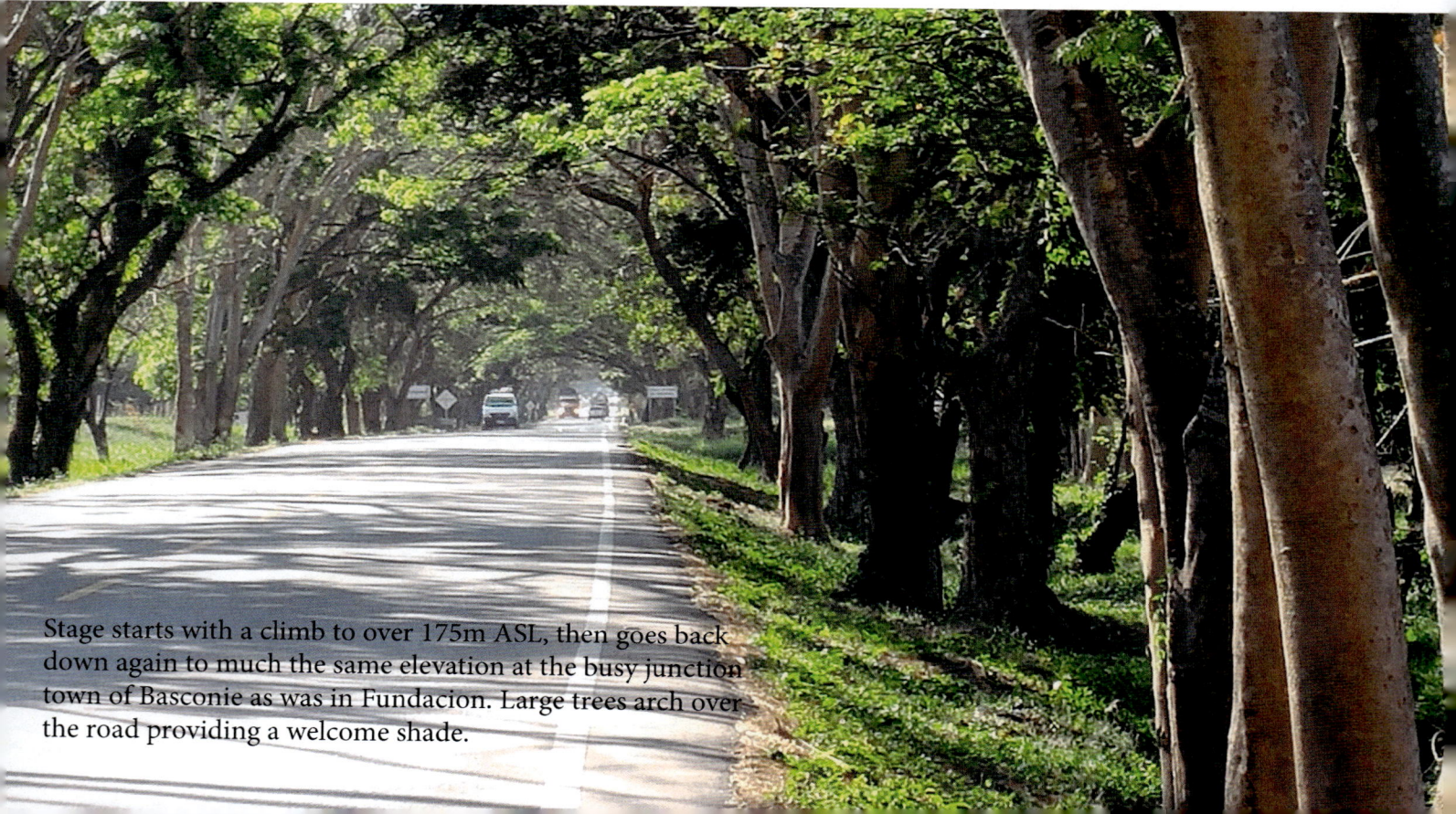

Stage starts with a climb to over 175m ASL, then goes back
down again to much the same elevation at the busy junction
town of Basconie as was in Fundacion. Large trees arch over
the road providing a welcome shade.

6. BOSCONIA TO CURUMANI

Distance: 100 km
Altitude Profile (34 m to 97 m)

Easy stage, all gradual, downhill or uphill, but hot. On the road at 5 AM, the heat is tolerable until 9 AM, then it hits you mercilessly: 105F in the shade by 10, 120F on the sun by noon. And trucks: this many was not usually the case; at least they headed in the opposite direction than I and there was an ample shoulder.

Right: Drive with caution, animals crossing!

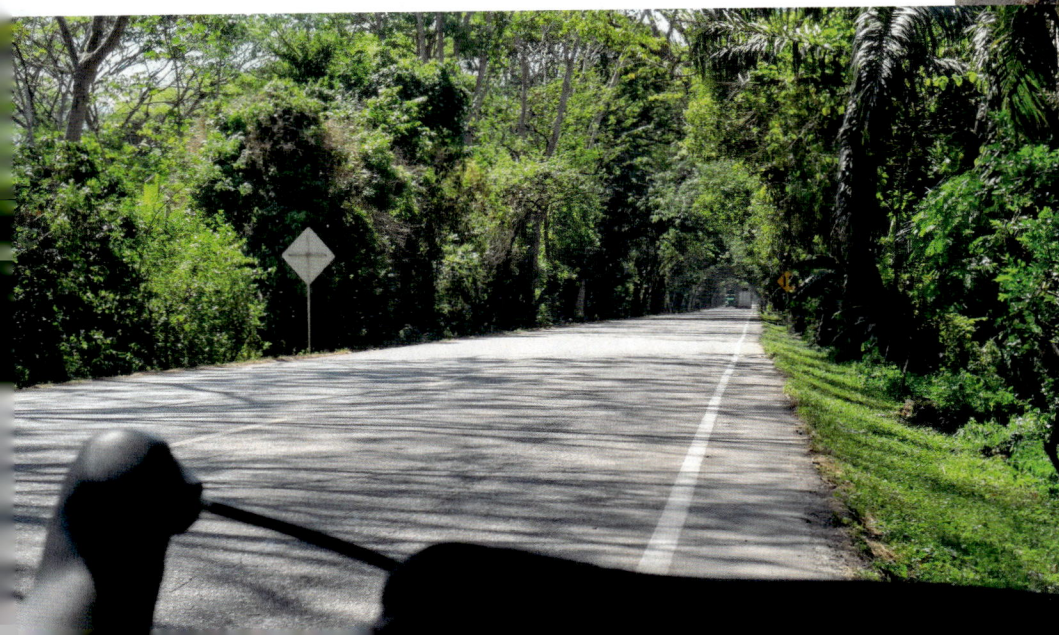

Left: Heavy vegetation cover along the highway near San Roque

7. CURUMANI TO PELAYA
Distance: 68 km
Altitude Profile (30 m to 94 m)

One steep hill, level from there.
Above: Keeping on schedule, on the road at
5 AM. Nice shoulder most of the way.

Right: A sign warns of Divided Highway
ahead, "Inicio Double Calzada." The shoulder is wide, the tarmac is perfect, and the
traffic is nil; what more can you ask?

Above left: Pelaya, another busy agricultural market town with corn and livestock the main commodities.

Above right: Trucks go by until late at night in Pelaya and first stalls open when it's still dark and I get on my way cycling to Aguachica.

Left: Now warning about monkeys; before it was ant-eaters, snakes, lizzards..., whatever; so far I haven't even seen a mosquito ...

Below: First stall open at 4:30 AM in Pelaya.

8. PELAYA TO AGUACHICA
Distance: 46 km
Altitude Profile (58 m to 294 m)

Not a long day's ride but a steady climb from 25m ASL to 300m ASL, a taste of the climb to Bucaramanga awaiting ahead. The heat remains as bad as ever.

Above: Panorama of the Cordillera Oriental from the road approaching Aguachica

Left: Crossing a small creek surrounded by a patch of lush jungle. While the scenery suggests a profusion of tropical vegetation, the hillsides are parched, the ground cover mere scrub mostly yellow-dry this time of the year, but still a nice scenery to pause for a few minutes.

Left: Looking back toward Norean on top of the hill, about 10 km before Aguachica. The downhill follows a long uphill just as the temperature is rising.

9. AGUACHICA TO SAN ALBERTO

Distance: 69 km
Altitude Profile (84 m to 187 m)

Another easy stage, leading slightly downhill then all flat until San Alberto.
Below: Mid-morning stop for a cup of "tinto" (black coffee), arepas or empanadas. If you do this every day, you will learn to taste the difference and appreciate the quality. Just as only one out of 10 tintos is superb, same goes for the culinary staples of Colombia.

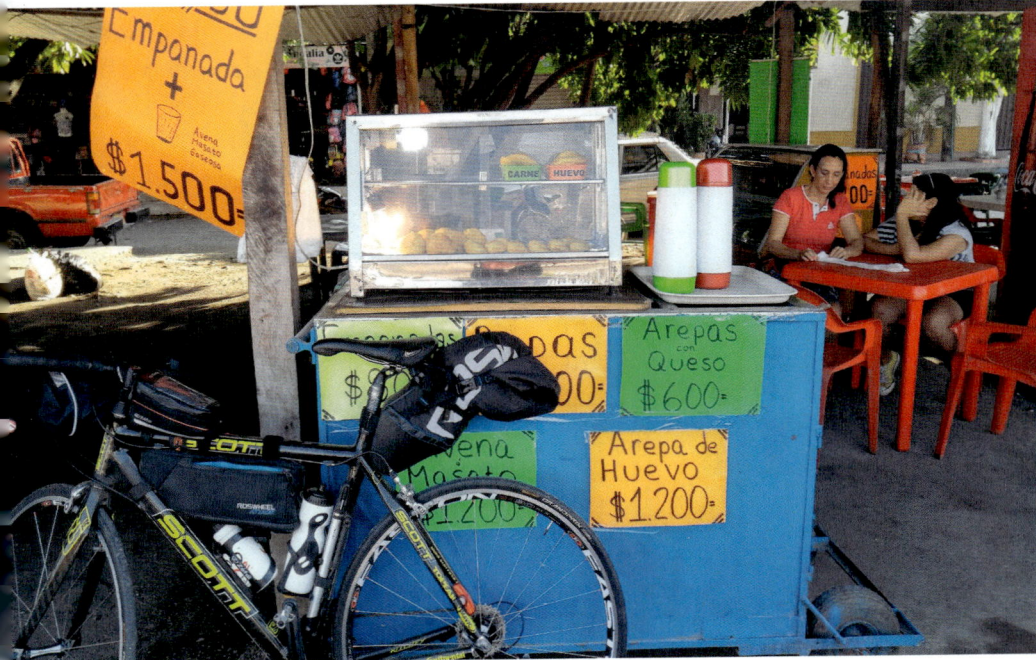

10. SAN ALBERTO TO EL PLAYON

Distance: 53 km
Altitude Profile (103 m to 772 m)

Into the mountains at last: a steady climb with three hills; gaining elevation. It's a tough going after all the days in the plains. The benefits are fine views, impressive vegetation, and cooler temperatures.

The stage from San Alberto to El Playon is one of the most scenic of the tour of northern Colombia. The views are often magnificent and the vegetation refreshing.

There is a significant change in traffic. Just before San Alberto the highway 45 divides. Taking the right you continue on the 45 which carries on through the plains. For much of the way until Honda, the 45 follows Rio Magdalena. The trucks heading to Bogota take this route as it saves them the ordeal driving the long, steep and winding road through the Cordillera Oriental range of the Andes, preferring the short albeit steep climb from Honda to get into Bogota.

Heading to Bucaramanga, the 45 becomes 45A. The only reason for the trucks or anyone to take it is when going to the capital of Santander. While the truck traffic never ceases, at least those that you will encounter on the road labor slowly up the steep inclines just as you do and don't whizz by at great speeds

With more refreshing climate, a variety of fruits grow in the hills and mouth-watering fruit stalls line the road..

After three climbs for the day, the last twenty kilometers you will lose the elevation gained, and as you come close to El Playon, the trucks become menace once again.

11. EL PLAYON TO BUCARAMANGA

Distance: 50 km
Altitude Profile (429 m to 959 m)

There are four hills, four climbs, each followed by a downhill; a maximum elevation of nearly 1,000 meters ASL is just before Bucaramanga. The scenery is much the same as the day before until you get close to the big city. Late morning and not too far to go, I stopped at this roadside parrilla, a grill restaurant in Rio Negro. Slabs of beef, pork, chicken, and guts were sizzling; I settled for two "chorizos," sausages and an arepa.

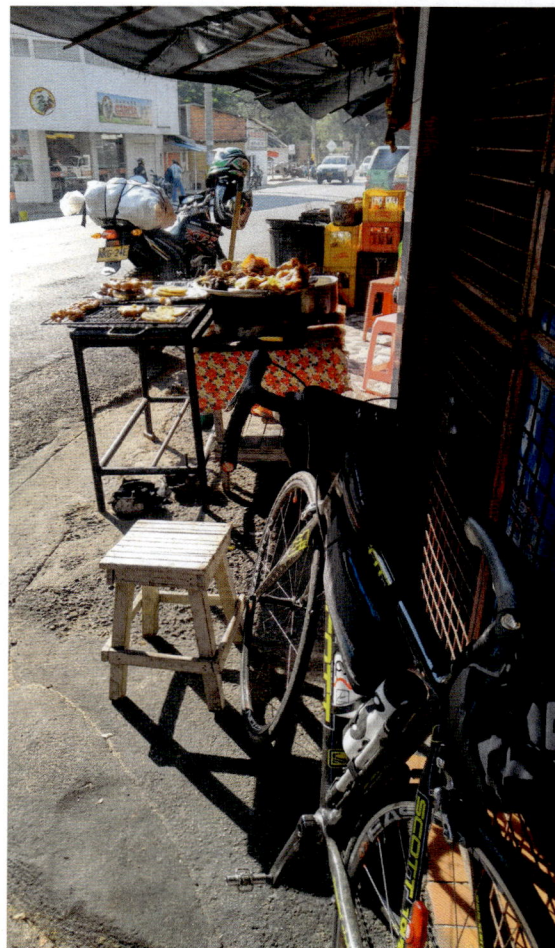

Above: Old Town plaza of Giron.
Right: Sunday ciclovia at Bucaramanga

12. BUCARAMANGA TO MOMPOX

Distance: 225 km

Going to Mompox means having to backtrack to north of Pelaya, a long way, even if the first part is all downhill. The turnoff for highway 78 for Mompox is at El Burro. It is 150 km from Bucaramanga and nowhere to stay here; you can overnight at Pelaya again. El Burro to Mompox is 74 km, the landscape scrub grassland (below). The 78 is paved until El Banco. From just before Guamal (right), the road becomes pure hell: six inches deep layer of fine sand, clouds of thick dust every time a motorbike passes, not to mention a truck or a bus. Not a surface for a road bike with thin 25C tires. I opted for a bus. After Guamal, the tarmac returns starting at the Pamban Bridge, where the highway 78 crosses to the south side of the Brazo de Mompos. The pavement is not new and is potholed severely the rest of the way.

MOMPOX

Cycling along the Brazo de Mompos, an arm of the Rio Magdalena between five and six in the morning, you can have this colonial gem of a small town all to yourself. The long shadows make the vibrant colors of the facades mesmerizing. Only a handful of tourists make it to Mompox which makes the experience so much more special.

By seven, a few locals gather at street corners, a pineapple seller will spread his goods at the riverbank. Cycling the waterfront is an unforgettable experience. By 8:30 AM the sun rises, the shadows change, the colors become less vivid and more people frequent the riverside. The early show at dawn is over. Gradually the sun rises higher and the heat bakes the colonial architecture until late afternoon. The streets stay busy until just past noon. At that hour, the streets empty as it becomes too hot for most, and the siesta begins. Late afternoon, the activities resume and after dusk the street carts roll out on the plazas and Mompox teems with life.

Early dawn at the Iglesia Santa Barbara in Mompox

Above: Eary morning at the riverbank in Mompox

Right: Morning meat market under a banyan at the village of Santa Ana, west of Mompox en route to ferry bound for Magangue.

13. MOMPOX TO SAN PEDRO
Distance: 99 km
+477 m / -337 m

Rio Magdalena is as much as a mile wide and although a bridge is under construction, the only way to cross it (2018) is by ferry. Do not take the car and truck ferry! It is cheaper but slow. Take one of the speedboats (lancha); they depart from a pier left of the ferry landing and take around thirty minutes to do the crossing. Seeing the guy tie my bike on the roof, I was concerned if my steed would make it to the other side as his knots seemed lame. But it did; my bike wasn't the first bike he handled. Managuue port is busy and erratic. It spews mad traffic into congested center of town right at the riverfront. Getting off the boat at high noon I succumbed to the stifling heat. To escape it, I sought the cooler interior of the Catedral Nuestra Señora De La Candelaria nearby for a short relief. A local with a bike who appeared to have come for the spiritual reasons was already there, hence I pedaled right in. Frankly, you don't leave your bike outside, assuming it will be there when you have satisfied your needs inside the church; remember, this is Colombia!

Left: The road from Magangue to San Pedro is bumpy on account of a rough gravel embedded in tarmac, but there is no traffic; pastures and cattle ranches line the road on both sides.

Below: San Pedro is a pleasant small town sporting interesting colonial vernacular house architecture.

14. SAN PEDRO TO EL CARMEN DE BOLIVAR
Distance: 68 km
+612 m / -589 m

From San Pedro, the stage leads up and down into the Maria Hills, to the highest elevation over 300 meters ASL, then down to half the altitude at Carmen de Bolivar, a busy highway junction town.

The three images in this spread are from the Los Palmitos area of highway 78 just before the junction with highway 25. The landscape is hilly with large trees arching over the highway. This is the southern part of the Montes de María, better known as Serranía de San Jacinto further north around the town of San Jacinto. The Maria Hills make up the northern-most extension of the West Andes. The rugged hilly region was in the relatively recent years prone to FARC and Paramilitary clashes. It is now calm. There may be a few soldiers patrolling the junction with highway 25, a reassuring sight for one's peace of mind.

More trucks ply the Highway 25 as this road is the Panamericana, the principal road from Cartagena to Medellin and further south. Compared to the 45 from Barranquilla/Santa Marta to Bogota, there is never a shoulder on 25, not even a sliver. As significantly more traffic streams to Medellin from Bogota than from Cartagena, there is less traffic on 25 than on 45, however.

Carmen de Bolivar is a quiet town. All the action is at the road junction of 25 and Highway 80 that leads to Bosconia and Valledupar in the far east. Hotels, hospedajes, bars and eateries line the road, providing for a great spectacle.

15. EL CARMEN DE BOLIVAR TO SAN JACINTO

Distance: 17 km
+266 m / -189 m

A short ride, staying in the hills, keeping to an elevation of around 300 m ASL with a downhill into town (below). Having a few days left before needing to be back in Cartagena, I spent the rest of my time in San Jacinto and San Juan Nepomuceno. It was a good decision. No tourists come to these small towns. San Jacinto may see a handful of music buffs a year on account of its native cumbia group Los Gaiteros de San Jacinto having become the winner of the Latin Grammy Award.

San Jacinto is a lively town. Every evening literally the entire town shows up on its plaza, fills the panaderias, bars, restaurants and every establishment around its perimeter. People chat, drink and eat until late at night.

Above: Mobile coffee-man with his thermoses comes to the sidewalk in front of the police station. People are friendly, cops included.

Left: The regional museum is a fine colonial building and not to miss for a glimpse of the unique culture in the Maria Hills.

16. SAN JACINTO TO SAN JUAN NEPOMUCENO

Distance: 20 km
+103 m / -182 m

Soft-pedal to another small town. Leaving the hills, the road leads downhill from San Jacinto, dropping 300 metres in elevation to almost sea level.

Below: At the Iglesía Central named after him, find the statue of the Bohemian Saint John of Nepomuk. Confessor of the Queen, he was drowned at the behest of the King for refusing to divulge the secrets of the Queen's confessional. By now I was comfortable to ride right into the house of God, at least in Colombia.

Left: On the church plaza stands the San Juan City Hall, a fine colonial edifice.

Left below: In the heat of the day, the town shuts down and may become a one-horse town. But in the evening (below), it comes alive again. San Juan Nepomuceno provides a great insight into life in a small town. There is no specific reason to come here other than for the slice of real Colombia. There is nothing to do, just walk the streets in the morning, rest at siesta, and watch the traffic go by with a bottle of beer in your hand in the evening.

17. SAN JUAN NEPOMUCENO TO TURBACO

Distance: 73 km

+475 m / -466 m

An enjoyable ride through the hills to a ridge of 200 m ASL at Turbaco overlooking the sea coast. Soon after San Juan, you leave the 25 which continues to Barranquilla. Instead, you pick up Highway 90 for a straight shot to Cartagena.

With one more day to spare, I cycled to Turbaco, just a hop from Cartagena. An easy stage, I dropped into a roadside restaurant to sample their assortment of staple delicacies and the inevitable cup of "tinto." It was an excellent one and saw a steady stream of customers. Soon after, I crossed the lagoon (above), one of many that are part of the wide Rio Magdalena estuary. I felt confident on my bike by this point of the journey. I defied the trucks treading the fine white line of a pavement. They skirted the line close when I stood off the tarmac but gave me an extra room when passing, most of them respectful. My trip was coming to a close, and I was well aware staying safe was important until the end. I took no chances but stood my ground.

18. TURBACO TO CARTAGENA

Distance: 19 km
+20 m / -204 m

All downhill from Turbaco, from 200 m ASL to sea level, then fighting traffic in the Cartagena rush hour.

STAGES AND DISTANCES

In the table below, find the summary of the stages and their respective distances.

Per the table, the total distance of the trip was 1,320 km, Cartagena back to Cartagena, in 18 travel days, 17 days by bicycle and one day in part by bus.

I spent 35 days in Colombia on this trip, eight of those in Cartagena (five nights at the front end, three nights at the tail end), a week in Bucaramanga, four nights in Mompox, and an extra day at some other places. The essence of my trip was still sightseeing and visiting friends, not a bike race.

By the time you read this, the road to Mompox may be all new and then you can ride your bike all the way.

STAGE	KM
Cartagena to Puerto Colombia	109
Puerto Colombia to Cienaga	96
Cienaga to Rodadero / Santa Marta	43
Rodadero/Santa Marta to Fundacion	92
Fundacion to Bosconia	73
Bosconia to Curumani	100
Curumani to Pelaya	68
Pelaya to Aguachica	46
Aguachica to San Alberto	69
San Alberto to El Playon	53
El Playon to Bucaramanga	50
Bucaramanga to Mompox	225
Mompox to San Pedro	99
San Pedro to El Carmen de Bolivar	68
El Carmen de Bolivar to San Jacinto	17
San Jacinto to San Juan Nepomuceno	20
San Juan Nepomuceno to Turbaco	73
Turbaco to Cartagena	19
18 DAYS – Total kilometers	1320

ACCOMMODATIONS

With lodging accounting typically for the highest of your daily expenses, I provide a table showing the name and price of the accommodations I used.

I booked no accommodations ahead of time other than in Cartagena before my arrival. In Cartagena, I booked a room through Airbnb. All the other hotels, hostels and hospedajes I picked as I rode past them.

In my table I provide a brief assessment of each, though

I do not profess there may not be a better place where to stay at each stop along the itinerary, at some locations I am certain of having found the best as the choices were only a handful.

My opinion on lodging is not too conventional. I am not too concerned where I stay unless I need to stay there for a few days. All I care about is having a shower and toilet, and the rest is secondary. I will shower and spend the rest of my time outside, then return to sleep, get up and leave, so having nice furnishings or a view is not too important. Colombians maintain their living quarters with care and even an inexpensive lodging with dated furnishings is immaculately clean. All the accommodations I stayed at were fine although some were better than others.

Following is my lodging list along with a price per night and a brief evaluation.

I show the costs in USD based on an approx. rate of exchange $1 equals 2900 Colombian peso as applied during my visit. All payments were in cash other than where I noted I could pay by credit card if accepted.

All rooms came with private bathroom, TV, and air-con unless I show otherwise.

Following the table I provide a few pictures for illustration. You can find more photos of the accommodations I used in my Flicker albums (see LINKS TO RESOURCES).

I always insist on keeping my bicycle in my room, a request not in many countries appreciated or granted, regardless of the accommodations standard. Not an issue in Colombia, however. Colombians are well aware bicycles cost a lot of money and have no problem if you want to keep your bike in your room.

LOCATION	PROPERTY	COST
Cartagena	Airbnb Host L. Daniel	Eur17.09/n +Eur10.48 service fee
	(convenient location though not in the Old Town but in the commercial center; nice guy, no aircon, horrible mattress, poorly maintained cluttered shared bath with two female Colombian students, terrible filthy kitchen, poor value accommodation)	
Puerto Colombia	Kasamar Hostel (4-bed dorm room)	35,000 / $12
Cienaga	Hotel Diamante Real (excellent)	50,000 / $18.51 by CC
Rodadero	Hotel Caribe Real (fair)	40,000 / $13.79
Fundacion	Hotel Milan (rustic building, rustic room but immaculate, enjoyable stay)	35,000
Bosconia	Hotel Ejecutivo (a bit funky, noisy market)	40,000
Curumani	Hotel Mayumir (wonderful place, pleasant woman owner, Eilses; loved coffee as much as me; without my asking served me a free cup several times a day)	40,000

Pelaya	Hotel Parqueadero (hot room despite air con; lower quality compared to previous; lower value)	35,000
Aguachica	Hotel Chalet (a big bed that could sleep 5!)	40,000
San Alberto	Hotel Belyferwis at the el parque (good value)	35,000
El Playon	Hotel Coco (no air-con, fan only; endurable as it was inside a cool inner courtyard with good restaurant in the front)	25,000
Bucaramanga	Hotel Preferencial Class (excellent value, incl breakfast, well run, nice staff)	50,000 / $18.22 by CC
Mompox	Hotel Santa Cruz de Mompox (no aircon but OK as on lower inner-courtyard level)	25,000
San Pedro	Hotel Dany (right price, expected standard)	35,000
El Carmen de Bolivar	Hospedaje in the market; fan only; just acceptable	24,000
San Jacinto	Hotel Casablanca (nice place, in vale about same as the 40,000 places earlier but no better choice in town)	50,000

San Juan Nepomuceno	Hotel Imperial (well run, good place)	40,000
Turbaco	Hospedaje (no aircon, poorly furnished, poor value, high price likely on account of the proximity to Cartagema)	40,000
Cartagena	Airbnb Host L. Daniel (poor value, not recommended)	Eur20.51 + Eur2.57 Airbnb service fee

Above: Hotel Milan, Fundacion

Below: Hospedaje, El Carmen de Bolivar

Above: Hotel Chalet, Aguachica; bed that sleeps 5

Right: Hotel Imperial, San Juan Nepomuceno

Below: Hotel Belyferwis, San Alberto

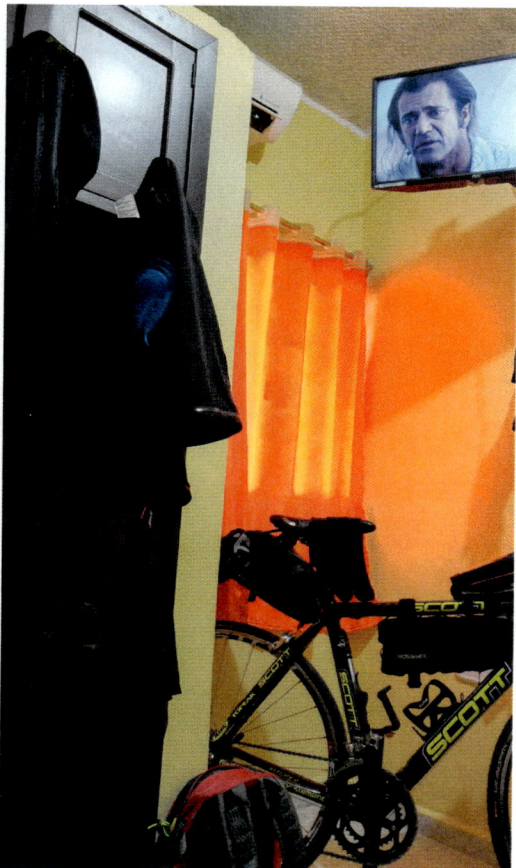

Right: Airbnb room in Cartagena; time to pack the bike ...

LINKS TO RESOURCES

Download my GPX tracks using the following direct link. It will take you to my Google Drive folder titled Cycling Northern Colombia GPS:
https://goo.gl/SV4Jq1

For an extensive photographic coverage of the trip, go to my Flickr Collections site:
https://goo.gl/m7e2fS

Follow me on Instagram:
https://www.instagram.com/footloosecycling/